# JUDAS

## A LENTEN DRAMA

Sharon Thompson

JUDAS
A LENTEN DRAMA

© 2022 Sharon Thompson

Published by
Texianer Verlag
Tuningen
Germany

www.texianer.com

ISBN: 978-3-94917-95-6

Cover illustration:
*The Kiss of Judas (between 1304 and 1306) by Giotto di Bondone depicts Judas' identifying kiss in the Garden of Gethsemane (public domain – PD-US).*

# Table of Contents

INTRODUCTION..................................................................5

A NOTE ABOUT THE PRODUCTION............................11

CAST OF CHARACTERS....................................................13

JUDAS...................................................................................15

    Scene 1................................................................................17
    *Pilate's Residence at Caesarea, 26 A.D.*
    Scene 2................................................................................21
    *A few days later, near the Jerusalem temple*
    Scene 3................................................................................23
    *Pilate's residence, days later*
    Scene 4................................................................................25
    *An office near the stadium*
    Scene 5................................................................................27
    *Stadium at Caesarea*
    Scene 6................................................................................31
    *A Street corner in Jerusalem*
    Scene 7................................................................................33
    *Near Bethany, the Sunday preceding Passover, 36 A.D.*
    Scene 8................................................................................37
    *The Council Chambers*
    Scene 9................................................................................43
    *Gamaliel's House*
    Scene 10..............................................................................47
    *John's House*
    Scene 11..............................................................................49
    *Caiaphas' Residence*
    Scene 12..............................................................................51
    *John's House*
    Scene 13..............................................................................53
    *A Secret Meeting Place*
    Scene 14..............................................................................57
    *Caiaphas' Residence*

Scene 15..................................................................................61
*John's House*
Scene 16..................................................................................65
*Pilate's Residence in Jerusalem, Friday Morning*
Scene 17..................................................................................67
*The Balcony of Pilate's Residence*
Scene 18..................................................................................69
*The Temple, Friday Morning*

WORKS CITED......................................................................71

# INTRODUCTION

I recently attended a performance of Peter Shaffer's play, *Equus*. The play was inspired by an irrational crime—a young man had intentionally blinded a number of horses with a sharp object. The playwright knew nothing about this individual or the circumstances surrounding the crime—only of the crime itself. The play seeks to create a mental world where the crime can be made comprehensible.

This short drama is of the same nature. We do not really know Judas: we only know his crime. What could make the crime of Judas comprehensible? We have limited information about Judas. He was from a Judean village, Kerioth; he was one of the twelve disciples of Jesus of Nazareth, the only non-Galilean. He was appointed treasurer of the group; he betrayed Jesus into the hands of the Jewish authorities and subsequently committed suicide. Since we do not know the "real" Judas, or never will, his characterization must, of course, be imaginary. This drama is an attempt to present one possible set of circumstances that could have motivated Judas to act as he did.

I have attempted to remain true to the historical people and circumstances involved as we know them from the New Testament and other sources. The obvious exception to this is Jesus Barabbas. In this instance I have based my portrayal on an interpretation by Robert Eisler. This view, although unorthodox, has strong critical support.

> *The support which he (Barabbas) received from the high priests and mass of followers strongly suggests that he was a well-known partisan of the hierarchy, the son of an Abba (Father) or Rabban (Master), both words designating a venerable doctor of the law, connected not with the rebels, but with their opponents, who in the melee had been captured along with them and now was destined to share their punishment. If it was a case of mistake on the part of the Roman guard, such as would often occur in every tumult of this kind, then Pilate, yielding to the voice of the people, might well have liberated him "for the feast", i.e. with such dispatch that the innocent man might still take part in the Passover celebration. But to pardon a known and condemned rebel was notoriously beyond the power of a Roman governor, and by doing so he would have been guilty of an invasion of the prerogative of the emperor such as the suspicious Tiberius would have been the least to tolerate. No one, in fact, has hitherto succeeded in discovering an illustration in Jewish or pagan writings of the alleged Jewish custom of obtaining pardon for a prisoner at the Passover* (Eisler 473).

The name of the man known as Barabbas, or Jesus Barabbas, comes down to us in two forms, Bar-Abba and Bar-Rabban. Bar means "son of", while Abba means "Father" and Rabban means "Master". Thus, the meaning of the names are "Son of the Father" and "Son of the Master". These two names are descriptive rather than the actual name of this person whose given name was Jesus, a common Jewish name of that time.

Can the illustrious parent of Jesus Barabbas be identified? Gamaliel is a logical guess. The honorary position of deputy of the high priest was customarily held by a

Pharisee. He was known as Abba Beth-Din (Father of the Court of Justice) and was also given the title Rabban (Master). Rabbinical tradition states that this office was bestowed on the leading Pharisee, Gamaliel, at about this time. Although only conjecture, the strong possibility exists that Gamaliel (Father of the Court of Justice) and Barabbas (Son of the Father) were, in reality, biological father and son.

The evidence of his name, the strong support he received from the chief priests for his release, and the fact that, indeed, he was released while those jailed with him for revolutionary activities were executed, strongly suggests that Barabbas was the son of a prominent Jew, who, for one reason or another, was mistakenly arrested and jailed. He could very possibly have been mistaken for Jesus of Nazareth who bore the same given name. It can be further noted that the gospel of Mark (the other gospels are dependent upon his narrative) does not identify Barabbas as a revolutionary, but rather, speaks of him as being in jail with the revolutionaries.

Can Gamaliel and Barabbas reasonably be identified as secret supporters of Jesus? It was not unknown for prominent Jews to be secret supporters of Jesus as in the instances of Nicodemus and Joseph of Arimathea. We have the account in Acts 5 of Gamaliel speaking out in support of the release of Peter and the other apostles when the Council wishes to condemn them. Furthermore, the earliest apostolic tradition (Nazorean) claimed Gamaliel as a secret sympathizer, and as such, could warn the followers of Jesus about measures being planned against them by the chief priests.

Was there a Passover amnesty custom as alleged in the gospels? It would seem highly unlikely. The release of Barabbas by Pilate "for the Passover" would appear to be of quite another nature, as suggested by Eisler.

Why then is the Barabbas incident used as it is in the gospel story? The earliest gospel, Mark, was written shortly after the Jewish/Roman war and was written in Rome for non-Jewish Christians. The entire tone of Mark is anti-Jewish and pro-Roman. The use of the Barabbas incident is in line with this general policy of Mark—it allows "the Jews" to be blamed for the crucifixion of Jesus, while Pilate, the Roman governor, can appear to be completely innocent of the crime.

Arguing for this interpretation does not intend to imply criticism of the author of Mark. His was a monumental task. Persecution of the Roman Christians by Nero following the great fire had virtually eradicated that community. The apostolic church in Jerusalem, which included the family of Jesus, had either fled Jerusalem just prior to the Jewish/Roman war or were victims of the war. In any event, communication was severed. By this time, the leading apostle, Peter, had been martyred as had James the Just (brother of Jesus) leader of the Jerusalem church. Reliable information would have been difficult to obtain. The original meaning of the Barabbas incident could easily have been lost, allowing the author of Mark to use it as he best saw fit.

By the time the remaining gospels were written, the split between nascent Christianity and post-war Judaism was virtually complete. Thus, allowance has been made for the anti-Jewish bias that the gospel writers would naturally exhibit. The Jewish masses gladly heard Jesus; they did not reject his claim of being the Jewish Messiah and certainly did not demand his crucifixion. On the contrary, it was the popular belief that he was the Messiah that prompted the pro-Roman Jewish authorities to act against him, to arrest him in secret and to turn him over to the Roman authorities for crucifixion completely without the knowledge of the common people. Had the common people rejected him as the Messiah there would have been no need for the Jewish authorities to conspire against him or for the Romans to comply with those wishes.

The chronology of Passion Week follows that of the Gospel of John. The "last supper" on Thursday evening was not the Passover meal as John clearly states. The Passover meal would have been celebrated on Friday evening which was the beginning of the Passover Festival, thus the necessity of arresting and trying Jesus in such haste, so that he could still be executed on Friday before the festival began that evening.

I originally wrote this drama to discover whether or not the theory I had about Judas would fit into the historical events as recorded in the Gospels. It did so very nicely, but what was inadvertently brought to my attention as I wrote, and of far greater import, was the transformation of the conflict which led to the arrest and crucifixion of Jesus. During the compilation and editing of the New Testament, its authors had changed this conflict (intentionally or otherwise) from a class conflict between Jesus (who spoke for the oppressed Jewish masses) and the Jewish and Roman authorities (who spoke for the powerful and privileged of their respective societies) to an ideological conflict between the Jews in general and the newly emerging Christian church. The result of this error has had dire consequences for both Jews and Christians — the Jews in having to endure relentless and undeserved persecution by Christians and the Christians in misunderstanding the message and mission of Jesus.

This drama is not so much a quest to discover the "real" Judas as it is to discover the "real" Jesus. The problem that Jesus confronted in the first century is with us yet today: a ruling class (determined by wealth and access to power) still dominates and oppresses the poor masses. However, today it is on a global scale (due largely to the unprecedented power of transnational corporations) with the very survival of human life on the planet at stake. This offers a compelling reason to re-examine objectively the collection of writings known as the New Testament and to seek to discover the real message that Jesus proclaimed and its implications for a world desperately in need of healing. My hope is that this drama will help initiate this timely and important debate.

## A NOTE ABOUT THE PRODUCTION

PROPS: The following scenes are outdoor scenes and require no props: 2, 6, 7, and 13. Scenes 1, 3, 4, and 16 suggest an official atmosphere. A small, easily-moved table and as much seating as necessary around it would be appropriate. Benches or low stools, rather than chairs, would be preferable. Scene 5 suggests that a tribunal is used; one of the benches would suffice. Scenes 9, 10, 11, 12, 14, and 15 take place in private homes. Adequate seating is all that is necessary. Scene 8 is a meeting of the Jewish council. It was a group of 71 men with the high priest as the presiding officer. They sat in a semicircle with the high priest at the center and 35 members each to his right and to his left. Gamaliel should sit next to Caiaphas. The stage can be set up as the top of the semi-circle. Although there are only five speaking parts, other actors (the two disciples, Marcus, Anthony, and the townsmen, all with a change of costume) should sit in as council members. When speaking, the actors should speak as if addressing the entire council, unless they are speaking directly to another council member. The narrator should use a lectern. Actors should move props at the end of the scene, when necessary.

COSTUMES: The Narrator should be dressed in contemporary clothing. The Romans (Pilate, Philip, Marcus, and Anthony) should be dressed in togas. Pilate should also wear a red robe. The disciples and Jesus should be dressed as typical, lower-class Palestinians. The townsmen, the Council members, and Jesus Barabbas should be dressed more elaborately as indicative of their class in society.

STAGING: The lectern should be placed on one side of the stage area. All actors, except the Narrator, should enter and exit the stage from the side opposite the lectern. When not on stage, the actors should be seated in the orchestra pit, if available, or another location near the stage in order to take part in the crowd scenes. The crowd is to be heard, not seen.

LIGHTING: A spotlight only should be used whenever the Narrator is speaking. All lights should be turned off at the end of each scene designating a change in time or locale or both. As the Narrator introduces the various characters, they should be highlighted with a spotlight.

MUSIC: The music can be as elaborate or as simple as desired. The hymns can be sung as solos, by a choir, or by the audience. If sung by the audience, the words should be printed in a program or projected onto a screen.

# CAST OF CHARACTERS

NARRATOR

PILATE, the Roman governor

PHILIP, aide to Pilate

JACOB, a townsman

OBADIAH, a townsman

GIDEON, a townsman

MARCUS, a Roman official

ANTHONY, aide to Marcus

DISCIPLE I

DISCIPLE II

CAIAPHAS, the Jewish high priest

GAMALIEL, a council member

LEVI, a council member

JONATHAN, a council member

CALEB, a council member

JESUS BARABBAS, Gamaliel's son

JUDAS ISCARIOT JOHN

JESUS OF NAZARETH

CROWD (This includes all actors who are not on stage at the time.)

SETTING: Palestine in the first century A.D. Scenes 1 through 5 take place immediately following Pilates's appointment to the governorship of Judea and Samaria in the year 26 A.D. The remainder of the drama takes place 10 years later during the week preceding the Passover celebration.

# JUDAS

NARRATOR: Judas. Judas Iscariot. What does that name bring to your mind? If I were to ask for one word... just one word... to describe Judas, what would it be?

AUDIENCE: Response to question. (Narrator ad lib, if necessary.)

NARRATOR: Yes, I can hear you. Betrayer. The name Judas has become synonymous with the word, betrayer. We are reminded of it in the communion service. When the pastor recites the words, "In the night in which he was betrayed", the name Judas forms in our mind. The season of Lent cannot go by without the name and deed of Judas being mentioned... and people wonder, "How could he have done such a terrible thing?"

Scholars struggle to answer that question. Was he mentally ill and therefore not responsible for his actions? Was he trying to force a showdown between Jesus and Rome, assuming, of course, that Jesus would win? Did he think by doing this he could hasten the coming of God's kingdom on earth? Was he simply greedy? Was money the motivation? The possibilities go on and on. But there is one possibility that has never been considered. Suppose that Jesus had asked Judas to do what he did. Ridiculous? Maybe, and then again, maybe not. The drama today/tonight is going to explore that very premise—that Jesus requested Judas to betray him to the Jewish authorities. And when the drama is over, maybe the question of "Why?" will finally be answered. Maybe some of you will understand why Judas did what he did. But now, allow me to introduce you to the first character you will be meeting today/tonight. This is Pontius Pilate. The Roman emperor, Tiberius, has just appointed him governor of Judea and Samaria. He was one of a long line of insensitive, arrogant Roman rulers who the Jewish people were forced to endure. But then, on the other hand, the Jews were not an easy people to rule. The year is 26 A.D. and we find the new governor conferring with an aide.

## Scene 1

*Pilate's Residence at Caesarea, 26 A.D.*

PILATE: O.K. First thing. I want an additional garrison of soldiers stationed at Jerusalem.

PHILIP: Yes, sir.

PILATE: There have been reports of minor problems there. And minor problems can become major problems.

PHILIP: I agree, sir.

PILATE: I think we have to let those Jews know that we mean business.

PHILIP: Absolutely.

PILATE: I want a garrison... in full dress uniform and carrying the Roman standards... ready to march in the morning.

PHILIP: (obviously very nervous) May I make a suggestion, sir? These Jews... are well, uh... are kind of different.

PILATE: So?

PHILIP: It has always been a policy that the soldiers do

not bring the Roman standards into the city of Jerusalem. The Jews... they have a rather, uh, a rather odd religion... and well, we've, uh, we've found it easier, I mean more diplomatic, to just not get them all upset about little things that don't really matter. They have this law... something about graven images... they just don't like them, I guess.

PILATE: Nonsense! The Jews are part of the Roman Empire. They will abide by Roman law, just like everyone else.

PHILIP: They have their own law, sir. They're very fussy about it.

PILATE: If those Jewish barbarians had an ounce of common sense they would recognize their own stupidity. Roman law is the only way... mark my words... the only way there will ever be peace in this sorry world.

PHILIP: Yes, sir. I agree, sir, but the Jews...

PILATE: (not paying any attention to Philip) We must do our part to ensure enforcement of it. and it is my duty to see that those wretched Jews do. They should be grateful that we care about their welfare.

PHILIP: They're so touchy, sir. You just can't reason with them.

PILATE: So? Who has to reason with them? They have no army... they have no leader... there is absolutely nothing they can do about it. The Roman standards are going to be displayed in Jerusalem. It's that simple.

PHILIP: Sir, I really think it would be easier to just let them do things their own way... within reason, of course.

PILATE: Who are the Jews to decide whether the Roman standards should be displayed in Jerusalem?

PHILIP: The Jews have certain rights, sir. They're different.

PILATE: Different? They benefit as much as anyone else from Caesar's rule. It is only fitting that the image of divine Caesar be displayed for all his subjects.

PHILIP: I hope you're doing the right thing, sir.

PILATE: The standards will arrive during the night. No one will even know about them until it is too late.

---

NARRATOR: The standards did, indeed, arrive under the cover of darkness. We now meet three residents of Jerusalem as they make this startling discovery the next morning.

---

## Scene 2

*A few days later, near the Jerusalem temple*

JACOB: (coming onto stage) No! God forbid! It cannot be!

OBADIAH: (coming onto stage) Jacob, what is it? What's the matter?

JACOB: The standards! The Roman standards! There they are! Right over there (covering his eyes) I can't look! God forbid!

OBADIAH: Now just calm down, Jacob. There's been a mistake made. You know it's a mistake. Pilate just took office. Nobody told him that the standards are not to be displayed in Jerusalem. It's just a mistake.

JACOB: (apparently not listening) This can't be. It just can't be. God forbid.

GIDEON: (coming onto stage) What is it? What's happened?

JACOB: Don't look! Please, don't look! The Roman standards are displayed on the Fortress... within sight of the Temple. God forbid!

GIDEON: (angrily) What is the meaning of this? Have they no respect at all? Those heathens! Bringing their brass gods into the holy city! They should all die! Those filthy swine!

OBADIAH: Anger will get us nowhere. A simple explanation to Pilate is all that is needed. We will send a delegation to Pilate at once. Let's get the others and set out immediately.

NARRATOR: A sizable delegation of Jews set off for Caesarea to ask Pilate to remove the standards as policy dictated. Pilate's response was to totally ignore them for five days.

On the sixth day we look in on Pilate as he confers with an aide.

# Scene 3

*Pilate's residence, days later*

PHILIP: Sir, I really think... I mean, don't you think... I mean, really, sir, those Jews out there... they've been waiting for five days to see you. If you would just talk to them.

Really, sir, they've been waiting a very long time.

PILATE: You act as though I'm the one who has done something wrong. They are the ones who refuse to honor Tiberius. I would be remiss if I did remove the standards. I would be failing to show my proper respect. The standards will stay and that's final.

PHILIP: But, sir, they've been waiting so long... it's been five days now.

PILATE: I suppose the only way to get rid of those peasants is to meet with them.

They're as stubborn as a pack of mules.

PHILIP: You won't be sorry, sir.

PILATE: Have them assemble in the stadium.

PHILIP: Yes, sir.

PILATE: Bring in enough soldiers... say, three hundred... enough to surround them at least three deep.

PHILIP: Uh, yes, sir.

PILATE: Tell the soldiers that at my signal... let's see... I'll raise my right arm... tell them they should all draw their swords. Well, get on with it.

PHILIP: Yes, sir. Right now, sir.

---

NARRATOR: The flurry of activity in the stadium does not go unnoticed. We now look in on some seasoned Roman officials.

# Scene 4

*An office near the stadium*

MARCUS: (as if looking out a window) What's going on out there? Why are those troops assembling in the stadium?

ANTHONY: I have no idea. Let me get Philip. He should know. (leaves)

MARCUS: (still looking out the window) There's hundreds of them out there. Wait! There are some other people out there, too. It looks like... yes, it is... that delegation of Jews from Jerusalem.

PHILIP: (entering with Anthony) What is it you want, sir? I was told you wanted to see me.

MARCUS: Yes, I do. What's going on in the stadium? Why are those troops assembling out there?

PHILIP: (perplexed) I tried to tell him... but he just wouldn't listen. I know there's going to be trouble. I just know it.

MARCUS: Slow down, Philip. You tried to tell who, what?

PHILIP: Pilate. I tried to tell Pilate not to send the standards... but he did anyway.

MARCUS: Not to send the standards where?

PHILIP: To Jerusalem. He insisted on sending the standards into Jerusalem and, of course, the Jews are protesting, but he won't remove them and now he's threatening to kill all those Jews if they don't accept them.

MARCUS: He's what?

PHILIP: He's threatening to...

MARCUS: (interrupting) Yes, yes, I heard what you said. I just can't believe it. Someone has to stop him.

ANTHONY: He can't be allowed to kill those unarmed Jews.

MARCUS: I'm going out there. He has got to be stopped.


NARRATOR: We now move to the stadium where Pilate will exercise his sovereign power over his recalcitrant subjects. Or will he?

## Scene 5

*Stadium at Caesarea*

PILATE: (on tribunal, signals troops to draw swords) Whether you like it or not, you are under the authority of the divine emperor, Tiberius. You will receive the emblems of his divine authority in Jerusalem. Anyone continuing to object, will be executed.

CROWD: (ad lib) Then kill us! We will not transgress our law! We would rather die than break God's commandments! Which way is easiest? Shall we lie on the ground? Here, let us bare our necks! Well, get on with it!

MARCUS: (rushing up to Pilate) Sir, please listen! You've got to stop! There is no reason to provoke the Jews. You're being completely unreasonable.

PILATE: I'm being unreasonable? Just look at those people. They're insane... absolutely insane!

MARCUS: They're Jews. They have certain privileges... including no standards in Jerusalem. You should have been told this.

PILATE: As long as they're under my rule, they're the same as anybody else.

MARCUS: What are you going to do? Kill every last

one of them? If you harm one hair on their heads, every Jew in the Empire will protest. Tiberius will not stand for it. You have no choice... the standards have to go. You cannot leave them in Jerusalem.

PILATE: What is this world coming to? The crazy people are telling the rest of us what to do. (grudgingly to the crowd) O.K., O.K. The standards will go. (to himself) They're insane, absolutely insane. How can you rule madmen? (to Marcus) Get this scum out of here. They're making me sick.

---

NARRATOR: The imperial might and the military power of the Roman Empire were no match for the indomitable spirit of the Jewish people. Rome both scorned and feared the Jews whom she could not understand—an entire nation obsessed with the preposterous notion that they... and they alone... were God's chosen people. By keeping God's law, they were preparing themselves for the moment when God's kingdom would be established on earth. This would happen when the Messiah—God's chosen leader— would appear among them. All the nations, including Rome, would then be subject to Israel. Diligent study of their holy scriptures and a prophetic interpretation of history convinced these unusual people that their moment of destiny was at hand—the "Last Days," when God would send his Messiah, had finally arrived. Although the Jews were granted certain official privileges and the ruling elite lived a life of ease and luxury, the vast majority of Jews were poor peasants who endured a life of cruel oppression. They had now suffered for ten years under the harsh rule of the despised Roman governor, Pilate. How they longed for the day when God would send his Messiah. How they longed to be delivered from their oppression. And then it happened. Scattered rumors of the Messiah's appearance became a steady stream. Let's go to a street corner in Jerusalem and listen in on some local townsmen.

# Scene 6

*A Street corner in Jerusalem*

JACOB: Do you think the rumors are true?

OBADIAH: The rumors about what?

JACOB: The rumors about the Messiah. Everyone's talking about him.

OBADIAH: You mean the prophet from Galilee—Jesus of Nazareth?

GIDEON: He's from Galilee? What kind of a Messiah would that be?

OBADIAH: Let's not be too quick to judge. I've heard many good things about him.

JACOB: I've heard he heals the sick, and makes the lame walk. I know he's the one. I just know it.

GIDEON: How do we know for sure? Has he actually claimed to be the Messiah?

OBADIAH: It would be much too dangerous for him to make that claim in public. It is said he talks in parables so that the Romans won't understand the implications. If he is the Messiah, he will make it clear in his own good time.

GIDEON: Well, that can't happen soon enough for me. Those accursed Romans treat us like dogs. When the Messiah does come, they will get what they deserve. I can hardly wait.

OBADIAH: God will send the Messiah in his own good time. If it is Jesus of Nazareth, we will soon know.

NARRATOR: The people flocked to see and hear Jesus. They listened eagerly to his talk of God's kingdom where righteousness and justice would prevail. The last year of his ministry was a Jewish Sabbatical Year which happened to overlap the Roman tax year. This had a two-fold effect: it freed many people from the cultivation of the land to hear Jesus preach. It also intensified their hatred of the Romans as the people had even fewer resources than usual with which to pay the Roman tax. The more militant were only too eager to take up arms against the hated Romans. This already tense situation was about to deteriorate. Jesus planned to celebrate the Passover in Jerusalem. This festival, which commemorates the Jewish escape from Egyptian slavery, was sure to raise nationalistic fervor. As Jesus made his way south, his entourage swelled in size. They stopped to rest at Bethany. While there, Jesus sent two of his disciples on an unusual mission—he wanted a donkey. We now look in on these two unnamed disciples.

## Scene 7

*Near Bethany, the Sunday preceding Passover, 36 A.D.*

DISCIPLE I: A donkey?

DISCIPLE II: Yes, Jesus wants a donkey.

DISCIPLE I: But, whatever for?

DISCIPLE II: Well, how should I know? Hurry, you are to go with me.

DISCIPLE I: Where are we going?

DISCIPLE II: To the village entrance.

DISCIPLE I: And a donkey will just suddenly appear?

DISCIPLE II: (impatiently) There will be a donkey.

DISCIPLE I: (sarcastically) We're going to just happen to meet someone who is giving away donkeys?

DISCIPLE II: I said, "There will be a donkey."

DISCIPLE I: We just walk up and take someone's donkey.

DISCIPLE II: Arrangements have been made. If someone asks, we're to say, "The Lord has need of it." They will give us the donkey.

DISCIPLE I: You really think there is going to be a donkey?

DISCIPLE II: Yes, now come on. Let's get going. We've wasted enough time already.

---

NARRATOR: The disciples accomplished their task and returned with the donkey. As the large group of pilgrims assembled to leave Bethany for the ascent up to Jerusalem, Jesus mounted the donkey. The crowd looked on in disbelief. Riding into Jerusalem on a donkey could mean only one thing: Jesus was openly declaring, for the first time, that he was the Messiah — the Jewish king. Every Jew knew the Messianic passage recorded by the prophet, Zechariah: "Rejoice greatly, O daughter of Zion; shout, O daughter of Jerusalem: behold thy king cometh unto thee: he is just, and having salvation; lowly, and riding upon an ass, and upon a colt the foal of an ass." (Zechariah 9:9) The prophecy was being fulfilled before their very eyes. The Jerusalem-bound pilgrims were ecstatic. Mayhem reigned. The closer they got to Jerusalem, the more animated the celebration became. The people waved palm branches and spread their garments before Jesus their king. There was singing and shouting.

---

**MUSICAL INTERLUDE**

"All Glory, Laud, and Honor"
Verses 1-3

Scene 7

NARRATOR: The royal procession, led by Jesus enthroned upon the donkey, triumphantly reached the gates of Jerusalem and went directly to the temple. There, Jesus did the unthinkable — he drove the money-changers from their tables and disrupted their unscrupulous activity. Then he began to teach. The authorities had been alerted and they were there. They tried to entrap him as he spoke. They failed miserably and the crowd was only further convinced that Jesus was the Messiah. Word about Jesus spread throughout Jerusalem and to the pilgrims assembled near-by for the Passover celebration. Multitudes rushed to the temple to see and hear Jesus. Jesus had declared himself to be the Messiah and the common people welcomed him with eager hearts and open arms. However, for the ruling elite the reaction was quite different. They were responsible to their Roman masters for keeping the peace. Only recently, an anti-Roman riot had developed and lives had been lost — both Jewish and Roman. They could ill-afford to let this happen again. The crowds were becoming unmanageable. How would they go about controlling the near-riot conditions that were sure to get worse as the Feast Day approached? Let me introduce you to two members of the Jewish council. The first is Caiaphas, the Jewish high priest. As high priest, he was the presiding officer of the council. His family connections and wealth had gained him the position and his willingness to placate the Romans at any cost kept him there. What an insult to God-fearing Jews to be ruled by the likes of him. But enough about that old rascal. Let me introduce you to Gamaliel. Kind... gentle... loving... an upright and Godly man... a teacher held in high esteem by his students and loved by the people. As the leading Pharisee, the council had conceded to him the honorary position of deputy to the high priest. A rare man, indeed, but there was little he could do to counteract the duplicity and self-interest of the Sadducean majority on the council. We look in on the council now as they meet to discuss the explosive situation that Jesus of Nazareth has created.

# Scene 8

*The Council Chambers*

CAIAPHAS: You all know why we're here. This madman... what's his name? Gamaliel, you know.

GAMALIEL: Yes, Caiaphas. It's Jesus of Nazareth.

CAIAPHAS: Yes, that's it... Jesus. This Jesus and his Galilean henchmen... they've created a very serious problem. The simple-minded peasants actually believe that he is the Messiah, (sarcastically) They're ready to overthrow Rome.

LEVI: These religious charlatans... there ought to be a law against them... a new one turns up every time anti-Roman feeling is high.

JONATHAN: They are really quite harmless. The people will return to their labor next year. They will have neither the time nor the energy to follow strange teachers.

CALEB: Yes, and once the Roman tax collection is over, things will return to normal.

CAIAPHAS: Yes, I know that... but that doesn't help us for right now.

GAMALIEL: But you have heard Jesus yourself. He has

only the highest respect for the Law... he knows the scriptures forward and backward... he teaches responsibility to God and man...

CAIAPHAS: (interrupting) I don't care what he teaches. He's dangerous as long as the people imagine he's the Messiah. We can't allow another anti-Roman riot.

LEVI: The Zealots are sure to take advantage of the situation. Can't something be done about them?

JONATHAN: They think of themselves as the successors of Judas Maccabeus. I've heard them many times... their motto is: No ruler but God. They believe that God helps those who help themselves.

CALEB: They'll help all of us... right into a war with Rome. We simply cannot let that happen.

CAIAPHAS: We all know how easily a riot can develop. We were warned the last time. If we can't control the people, then Rome will do it for us.

LEVI: I agree with Caiaphas. We have to take care of our own problems or we will lose what little authority we still have to run our own affairs.

CALEB: I agree with you two. We have to be firm... for everyone's good.

CAIAPHAS: We have no choice. This Jesus must be silenced — permanently.

Scene 8

LEVI: What about his disciples? Shouldn't we get rid of them, too?

JONATHAN: Once the ring-leader is gone, his following will soon disappear.

CALEB: They're just Galileans. They're incapable of organizing any meaningful resistance.

CAIAPHAS: I agree. We need only to deal with this Jesus. The others are not a threat.

GAMALIEL: You are willing to condemn an innocent man?

CAIAPHAS: Surely, even you can see the danger that he poses. It is better that one man die than that the whole nation perishes. He must die before the feast begins.

GAMALIEL: What charges can you bring against him? He has broken no law.

CAIAPHAS: Maybe not any Jewish law, but Messiah means only one thing to the Romans... it means Jewish king and Jewish king means treason... an offense punishable by death.

LEVI: How will we precede against him? He is constantly surrounded by huge crowds.

JONATHAN: If we arrest him, the crowds will turn against us.

CAIAPHAS: No, the Romans must get the blame. We will convince them that Jesus has subversive intentions and if they don't do something immediately, they will be responsible for a full-scale riot. We have no power to effect the death penalty, anyway.

CALEB: That makes sense. The Romans aren't exactly deaf and blind. They can plainly see that there's a problem out there.

CAIAPHAS: The Romans will be more than happy to get rid of a Jewish trouble-maker. It is our duty to cooperate with them to protect our people. The, uh, untimely demise of one Jesus of Nazareth will benefit all concerned. It is only right that he should die for the nation. I will notify the Roman guard at once to be on the look-out for this Jesus.

---

NARRATOR: The council concluded their unpleasant, but necessary, business. And now, I must introduce you to another character in our drama—Jesus Barabbas, son of Gamaliel. In the gospel accounts, we know him only as Barabbas. However, in other sources he is also called Bar-Rabban and we learn that his given name is Jesus. If his given name is Jesus, then the other two names are descriptive and were used to help identify which Jesus he was. What do these names tell us about him? Bar means "son of", Abba means "Father", and Rabban means "Master". Thus, the meaning of the two names are "Son of the Father" and "Son of the Master". Gamaliel, because of his position as deputy to the high priest, was accorded the title Abba Beth-Din which

Scene 8

means "Father of the Court of Justice" and because he was a doctor of the law, he was given the title Rabban which means "Master". His son Jesus, therefore, was called Bar-Abbas (Son of the Father) and Bar-Rabban (Son of the Master). But why would the son of a prominent and highly respected Jew like Gamaliel be in the situation that we find him in the gospel accounts—imprisoned with two revolutionaries when Jesus is brought to trial? Hopefully, this will be explained to your satisfaction as our drama progresses. For now I will just say that Barabbas was a secret supporter of Jesus. He could supply Jesus with important information regarding the plans being made by the Jewish council of which his father was a member. We meet Jesus Barabbas now as he talks with his father, Gamaliel, following the council meeting.

# Scene 9

*Gamaliel's House*

JESUS BARABBAS: What is the news from the council, Father?

GAMALIEL: It is not good, my son. They have determined that Jesus must die... and that, before the feast.

JESUS BARABBAS: But they can't. They have no grounds. He has done nothing wrong.

GAMALIEL: Maybe not according to Jewish law. But, son, you must realize that many people are convinced that he is the Messiah, and...

JESUS BARABBAS: Father, he is the Messiah!

GAMALIEL: Yes, he may well be. But the timing... the timing is so incredibly bad.

JESUS BARABBAS: What charges will they bring against him? Claiming to be the Messiah certainly isn't a crime.

GAMALIEL: It is to the Romans. Caiaphas has notified the Roman guard that Jesus has subversive intentions. They are probably looking for him right now.

JESUS BARABBAS: They've turned their dirty work over to the Romans.

GAMALIEL: They are just being practical. The council can no longer pass the death sentence.

JESUS BARABBAS: They are willing to sacrifice Jesus to save their own stinking skins.

GAMALIEL: The crowds are getting unruly. A riot could break out at any time. They feel they are only doing their duty.

JESUS BARABBAS: Duty, indeed. They do not serve God or the people. All they care about are themselves and their positions.

GAMALIEL: They are to be pitied. They know neither the love of God nor the joy of serving their fellow man.

JESUS BARABBAS: And now they are plotting to kill the one person who can give that back to the Jewish people. Don't any of them realize what they are doing?

GAMALIEL: No, son. I'm afraid not. I have not been able to do anything to change their minds.

JESUS BARABBAS: I... I'm sorry, Father. I know how hard you've tried.

GAMALIEL: They see only crowds that have to be controlled and Romans that have to be appeased. They are caught in the middle.

Scene 9

JESUS BARABBAS: I have to go meet Judas. I must tell him the bad news.

GAMALIEL: Do be careful, son. There may be trouble on the streets already.

JESUS BARABBAS: If someone could just talk some sense to the crowds. I wonder... it's worth a try. I've got to do something.

GAMALIEL: Please be careful.

---

NARRATOR: And finally, we meet Judas Iscariot... better know as Judas, the Betrayer. Being the only non-Galilean of the twelve disciples, he served as the Jerusalem connection. He was familiar with the city of Jerusalem and knew many important people there. He was instrumental in making contacts for Jesus and for carrying out many essential details vital to the success of Jesus' well-laid plans. He was educated and was considered the "brains" of the disciple group while the hardy Galileans were considered the "brawn"–an effective bodyguard in dangerous times. There was little love lost between Judas and the Galilean disciples, but they each served a useful purpose. We meet Judas now as he waits at his friend John's house for the arrival of Jesus Barabbas. Barabbas will relay to Judas the outcome of the council meeting which he learned from his father, Gamaliel, and, in turn, Judas will pass that information on to Jesus.

# Scene 10

*John's House*

JUDAS: Why isn't Barabbas here yet? John, what do you suppose has happened to him?

JOHN: Relax, Judas. You know he will come. He's very dependable.

JUDAS: He should have been here by now.

JOHN: Maybe the council meeting ran late.

JUDAS: Not this late.

JOHN: Maybe Gamaliel was detained.

JUDAS: No. He knew how important it was that Barabbas meet with us.

JOHN: You're just going to have to wait until he gets here. Now, relax.

JUDAS: Jesus will want to know what the council is planning. I wish Barabbas would come.

JOHN: He will. Now just calm down.

JUDAS: I'm worried. Maybe something has happened.

JOHN: Nothing has happened. I'm sure he has a good reason for being late.

NARRATOR: We will leave Judas at John's house wondering why Barabbas is late for their appointed meeting and look in on Caiaphas at his residence.

# Scene 11

*Caiaphas' Residence*

CAIAPHAS: That was much easier than I thought it would be. We just received word—Jesus has been arrested.

LEVI: Was there any trouble with the arrest?

CAIAPHAS: No, none whatsoever.

LEVI: Have any other problems developed?

CAIAPHAS: Yes, unfortunately... but it has been minimal.

LEVI: What happened?

CAIAPHAS: A Roman soldier was killed. The two men responsible were arrested immediately. The rest of the crowd was dispersed peacefully, thank goodness.

LEVI: What happens now?

CAIAPHAS: Pilate will arrive early tomorrow morning. He will pass judgment. All of them—Jesus and the two murderers—will be executed before the feast begins in the evening. Who would have thought it would all go so smoothly?

JONATHAN: (bursting in, out of breath) Sir, I must talk to you immediately. We've made a mistake!

CAIAPHAS: A mistake? What kind of mistake?

JONATHAN: They've arrested the wrong Jesus. They have Jesus Barabbas in jail, not Jesus of Nazareth.

CAIAPHAS: Jesus Barabbas? How can that be?

JONATHAN: For some reason he was mixing with the crowds. The Roman soldiers came and they... they must have thought he was Jesus of Nazareth. He's in jail now with the two rebels who killed the Roman soldier.

CAIAPHAS: Somehow it just seemed too good to be true. What do we do now?

LEVI: Well, for starters, someone is going to have to tell Gamaliel about Jesus Barabbas.

JONATHAN: Do you think we can convince the Romans that they've made a mistake?

CAIAPHAS: I don't know... I just don't know. We don't have much time. If we could only get our hands on the real Jesus. God help us.

---

NARRATOR: We will leave Caiaphas and his cohorts to wrestle with their problem and return to look in on Judas. He is still waiting impatiently at John's house for the arrival of Jesus Barabbas.

## Scene 12

*John's House*

JUDAS: It's been hours. I just know that something has happened.

JOHN: There's someone at the door now. (answering door) Gamaliel! Come in.

GAMALIEL: I knew you would be worried about Barabbas.

JUDAS: Something's happened. I just know it.

GAMALIEL: Yes, I'm afraid so.

JUDAS: Well, what is it? Tell us.

GAMALIEL: Let me start at the beginning. The council determined that Jesus of Nazareth must die.. immediately. They notified the Roman guard..

JUDAS: But, they can't...

GAMALIEL: They can and they did. Jesus Barabbas was on his way over here... I'm not sure just what happened... there was a disturbance... my Jesus was involved in some way... they must have thought he was Jesus of Nazareth... at any rate, he was arrested and is being held in the Fortress.

JOHN: Is he in any danger? Surely the Romans can be convinced of the error.

GAMALIEL: They may or may not listen to us. They may think it is a trick of some kind.

JOHN: What can we do?

JUDAS: Jesus will know what to do. I'll go meet Jesus. He's waiting for me anyway.

NARRATOR: The final character in our drama is Jesus of Nazareth. An introduction hardly seems necessary. Yet somehow we have a tendency to think only of his skills as a teacher and his willingness to endure physical suffering and death. We fail to appreciate his brilliant mind and his strength of will, his ability to plan move and counter-move, to out-guess and out-maneuver his opponents. He would not be deterred—nothing, absolutely nothing—would keep him from seeing his purpose fulfilled. We meet him now as Judas informs him of the unexpected turn of events regarding Jesus Barabbas.

# Scene 13

*A Secret Meeting Place*

JUDAS: Jesus, I'm glad you're still here. I'm sorry I'm late, but there's been a problem.

JESUS: Tell me, Judas. I've been worried.

JUDAS: I was waiting for Barabbas at John's house and he never came. Finally, Gamaliel came instead. The Romans have arrested Jesus Barabbas and he's being held at the Fortress. (Jesus looks distracted) I told them that you would know what to do. Jesus, are you listening to me?

JESUS: Yes, I hear you. Just let me think, (more to himself than Judas) They probably mistook him for me. (to Judas) They will very likely execute him. We must do something.

JUDAS: But what? Gamaliel wasn't sure the Romans would believe him.

JESUS: They would have to if the real Jesus showed up.

JUDAS: You mean yourself?

JESUS: It is I whom they want. If they were to capture me, they would release Jesus Barabbas.

JUDAS: Do you know what you're saying?

JESUS: Yes, of course. The important thing is that Jesus Barabbas be released.

JUDAS: But what about you? These Romans are deadly serious.

JESUS: Trust me. Everything will work out.

JUDAS: But...

JESUS: Promise me you will help me.

JUDAS: But how? What can I do?

JESUS: We must act quickly. It will have to be tonight.

JUDAS: What will have to be tonight?

JESUS: You must go to the authorities. Most of them know you — they will trust you. You must convince them that... that you've finally come to your senses... that you realize now what a threat I am to the national safety. And being patriotic, you must do your duty. You are willing to cooperate in arresting me.

JUDAS: I... I don't know.

JESUS: You're the only one who can do it. It's our only chance to save Barabbas.

JUDAS: Yes, I can see that. But you will be placing yourself in a great deal of danger.

Scene 13

JESUS: I promise you that nothing will happen to me that is not according to God's will. Do you believe me?

JUDAS: Well, yes... of course. I... I'll do my very best.

JESUS: I know you will, Judas. I know I can count on you. You must go to see Caiaphas right away. Tell him that you will meet him immediately after the evening meal and that you will take him to me. I'll give you a signal when you should leave the meal. How about if I say, "What you are going to do, do quickly?"

JUDAS: (repeating) What you are going to do, do quickly. O.K., I've got that.

JESUS: You will meet us at Gethsemane at the usual place. You can identify me with a kiss of greeting.

JUDAS: O.K. (repeating) Gethsemane at the usual place... greet you with a kiss.

JESUS: You must hurry. I will see you at John's house for the evening meal. Do not tell a soul about this plan.

JUDAS: No, of course not.

NARRATOR: We return to look in on Caiaphas as he continues to wrestle with the problem he faces.

# Scene 14

*Caiaphas' Residence*

LEVI: (enters) Excuse me, sir. Judas Iscariot is here to see you.

CAIAPHAS: Judas who?

LEVI: Judas Iscariot. He says he must see you immediately.

CAIAPHAS: Tell him to go away. I have enough on my mind... what with Jesus Barabbas in jail and Pilate coining in the morning. Our only hope is to find this wily Jesus of Nazareth.

LEVI: But that's why Judas is here. He is willing to help us locate Jesus. He is one of his closest disciples.

CAIAPHAS: Well, why didn't you say so? Let me talk to the man.

LEVI: Yes, I'll bring him right in. (exits and returns with Judas)

JUDAS: I'm Judas Iscariot.

CAIAPHAS: Yes, I've heard of you.

JUDAS: Up to this time I've been a disciple of Jesus of Nazareth.

CAIAPHAS: Why do you say, "Up to this time?"

JUDAS: I'm a very patriotic person. At first I thought Jesus could help our people.

CAIAPHAS: And now?

JUDAS: Now I see what a threat he is to our national safety. The people are on the verge of rioting. The Romans will never allow that.

CAIAPHAS: You're a very smart man.

JUDAS: I feel it is my duty to cooperate in any way necessary to see that he is arrested.

CAIAPHAS: We have to have him yet today and it has to be done in secret. The crowds cannot know about this. Can you do that?

JUDAS: Yes, I can. Jesus will spend the evening in the Garden of Gethsemane. Only his closest disciples will be there. I can go with you and identify him.

CAIAPHAS: You're an answer to prayer. There will be something in this for you, of course. Is thirty pieces of silver enough to show our appreciation for your patriotism?

JUDAS: That is more than generous. I can meet you here immediately following the evening meal.

Scene 14

CAIAPHAS: I will notify the Roman guard. They will be here, also. You will not be sorry you did this, my good man.

NARRATOR: The initial phase of the plan to betray Jesus of Nazareth to the Jewish authorities in order to rescue Jesus Barabbas—or so Judas thinks—has been accomplished. Judas returns to John's house where he is to meet Jesus and the other disciples for the evening meal.

# Scene 15

*John's House*

JUDAS: (at the door) It is I, Judas.

JOHN: Yes, Judas, come in. You're late.

JUDAS: I had some... some business to attend to. Are the others here?

JOHN: Yes, they're all in the upper room. They're waiting for you.

JUDAS: May I rest for a moment? This has been a most trying day.

JOHN: You do look pale. Are you worried about Jesus Barabbas?

JUDAS: (covering up) Yes... yes, that's it. I'm worried about Barabbas.

JOHN: Jesus has taken his misfortune very hard. also. I hope everything turns out all right for him.

JUDAS: So do I. I'll be glad when Passover is over and we can leave Jerusalem.

JOHN: But then, Jesus takes everything so seriously.

It's like he has the weight of the whole world on his shoulders.

JUDAS: He is an exceptional man.

JOHN: He has been unusually quiet this evening. I think something is bothering him. I often wonder what he has on his mind.

---

## MUSICAL INTERLUDE

"Go to Dark Gethsemane"

Verse 1

(Accompaniment continues throughout the Scripture references below.)

JESUS OF NAZARETH: (from off-stage) The kings of the earth set themselves, and the rulers take counsel together, against the Lord, and against his anointed. (Psalm 2:2)

He is despised and rejected of men; a man of sorrows, and acquainted with grief: and we hid as it were our faces from him; he was despised, and we esteemed him not. (Isaiah 53:3)

I gave my back to the smiters, and my cheeks to them that plucked off the hair: I hid not my face from shame and spitting. (Isaiah 50:6)

He was oppressed, and he was afflicted, yet he opened

not his mouth: he is brought as a lamb to the slaughter, and as a sheep before her shearers is dumb, so he openeth not his mouth. (Isaiah 53:7)

Reproach hath broken my heart, and I am full of heaviness; and I looked for some to take pity, but there was none. They gave me also gall for my meat; and in my thirst they gave me vinegar to drink. For they persecute him whom thou hast smitten; and they talk to the grief of those whom thou hast wounded. (Psalm 69:20-21, 26)

All we like sheep have gone astray; we have turned every one to his own way, and the Lord hath laid on him the iniquity of us all. (Isaiah 53:6)

"Go to Dark Gethsemane"<br>Verse 1

NARRATOR: The betrayal in the Garden of Gethsemane went as planned. Jesus was arrested and the Jewish council brought charges against him during the night. It is now Friday morning and Jesus is scheduled to appear before the Roman governor Pilate at his Jerusalem residence.

# Scene 16

*Pilate's Residence in Jerusalem, Friday Morning*

PILATE: We have dealt with the two murderers. What is left?

PHILIP: There is another prisoner, sir... or rather, there are two prisoners, but there is really only one prisoner.

PILATE: You're talking nonsense.

PHILIP: It's all very confusing, sir. Two men were arrested for the same crime.

PILATE: And what is the crime?

PHILIP Treason against Rome, sir. The man claims to be the King of the Jews.

PILATE: Well, I can hardly try the case until I know which one he is, now, can I? Where are his accusers?

PHILIP: You will have to go to them, sir.

PILATE: What do you mean, "I'll have to go to them?"

PHILIP: The chief priests are the accusers. It is against their law, Sir, to enter a Gentile home on a Feast day. They refuse to come in.

PILATE: (sarcastically) Well, by all means, I shall go to them. I certainly wouldn't want them to break one of their precious laws. Where are they now? In the courtyard?

PHILIP: Yes. In fact there is quite a crowd assembled there. It looks like all the chief priests and most of their servants.

PILATE: Very well. Let's get this over with. Have them bring the prisoners to the courtyard as well. I will try the case from the balcony.

---

NARRATOR: We move from inside Pilate's residence to the balcony overlooking the courtyard. The fate of Jesus Barabbas and Jesus of Nazareth will be decided at this time.

---

# Scene 17

*The Balcony of Pilate's Residence*

PILATE: Which of these two men is accused of treason against Rome—Jesus Barabbas or Jesus of Nazareth?

CAIAPHAS: (as part of the crowd) Jesus Barabbas is innocent of any crime; release him at once.

CROWD: (ad lib) Release Barabbas! We want Barabbas! Barabbas!

CAIAPHAS: If you release him now, he can join his family for the Passover feast.

CROWD: (ad lib) Yes, release him for the feast! Release Barabbas for the feast!

PILATE: O.K., I hear you. Guards, release Jesus Barabbas. He is free to go. Then what shall I do with the man whom you call the King of the Jews?

CAIAPHAS: He is deserving of crucifixion.

PILATE: Why? What evil has he done?

CAIAPHAS: Every one who makes himself a king sets himself against Caesar. If you release this man, you are not Caesar's friend. You must crucify him.

CROWD: (ad lib) Let him be crucified! Crucify him! Crucify!

PILATE: I am innocent of this man's blood, see to it yourselves.

CAIAPHAS: His blood be on us and our children. Away with him. Crucify him.

NARRATOR: You all know the rest of the story. But have you ever given a thought to Judas during this time? Initially, he would have felt relief that his pretense had succeeded. But then what? The other disciples had fled during the arrest, fearing for their own safety. Had he been able to locate them, how could he explain what he had done? Who would have believed him if he had insisted that Jesus had masterminded his own betrayal? How did Judas spend the night? How and when did he learn the outcome of Jesus' trial? What was his reaction? It would be very different from that of the council members. We look in on them now as they are about to leave the Temple and go home for some much-needed rest.

# Scene 18

*The Temple, Friday Morning*

CAIAPHAS: Well, finally. I think we can put this matter to rest. Jesus Barabbas was released—just as we had hoped and Jesus of Nazareth was condemned to death—just as we had hoped. Two for two isn't bad.

LEVI: The Romans will carry out all three crucifixions immediately. The bodies will be taken down from the crosses before the festival begins this evening.

JONATHAN: Considering everything, we were pretty lucky. Maybe God does help those who help themselves.

LEVI: I think we can safely say that we nipped this crisis in the bud. Hopefully, this will discourage anyone else from declaring himself to be the Messiah.

CAIAPHAS: (stifling a yawn) Well, why don't we all go home and try to get a few hours sleep before the festival begins. (They all get up to leave.)

CALEB: (from off-stage, as he tries to restrain Judas) You can't go in there. They won't see you now.

JUDAS: I've got to. Let go of me.

CAIAPHAS: What's going on out there?

JUDAS: (breaks free of Caleb and enters) You've got to help me. I'm guilty. I have sinned in betraying innocent blood.

CAIAPHAS: How does that affect us? It's your concern. (Caiaphas and the others turn and walk away. Judas sinks to his knees in despair.)

## MUSICAL INTERLUDE

"Were You There When They Crucified My Lord?"
Verses 1-3

NARRATOR: Matthew concludes our story with these words: "And he cast down the pieces of silver in the Temple, and departed, and went and hanged himself". (Matthew 27:5) Four men died in Jerusalem on that fateful Friday. Three of them were executed as traitors against Rome; the fourth died by his own hand. You may continue to call Judas "betrayer", but you may well be referring to the ultimate act of human loyalty performed by a trusted and devoted friend.

# WORKS CITED

Bible verses from the King James Version. Nashville: Thomas Nelson Publishing, 1611.

Eisler, Robert. The Messiah Jesus and John the Baptist. London: Methuen, 1931.

www.ingramcontent.com/pod-product-compliance
Lightning Source LLC
LaVergne TN
LVHW090038080526
838202LV00046B/3865